QUESTION IT!

POPULATION
ARE THERE TOO MANY OF US?

PHILIP STEELE

WAYLAND

First published in Great Britain
in 2017 by Wayland
Copyright © Wayland, 2017
All rights reserved

Produced by Tall Tree Ltd
Editor: Jon Richards
Designer: Ed Simkins

ISBN: 978 1 5263 0335 6
10 9 8 7 6 5 4 3 2 1

Wayland
An imprint of Hachette
Children's Group
Part of Hodder and Stoughton
Carmelite House
50 Victoria Embankment
London EC4Y 0DZ

An Hachette UK Company
www.hachette.co.uk
www.hachettechildrens.co.uk

Printed and bound in China

The website addresses (URLs) included in this book were valid at the time of going to press. However, it is possible that contents or addresses may have changed since the publication of this book. No responsibility for any such changes can be accepted by either the author or the Publisher.

Every effort has been made to credit all photographs and illustrations correctly.

CONTENTS

IT'S TIME TO TALK ABOUT
POPULATION

People are everywhere. Motorways are jammed with traffic. Towns have grown into crowded megacities. Sometimes the planet seems to be as busy as an ants' nest, as humans scurry here and there. You even have to queue to climb Mount Everest these days. The population of Earth has been soaring for more than a hundred years. Is there enough room for so many people?

THE CHALLENGES

Most of the world's people are living healthier and longer lives than 100 years ago, and there are more and more of them. As a result, the population of the planet will face many new challenges in the coming years. Planet Earth is becoming warmer. Will there be enough food and water for so many people in an age of climate change? Are there enough resources to go around? How will population growth affect the environment? Already wars, natural disasters and poverty are forcing people to flee their countries and seek new homes. Will these movements of people add to the problems?

LIVES IN CRISIS
Many people are forced from their homes, either by natural disasters or war, and move to other countries as refugees.

NEWBORN
Around the world, more than 250 babies are born every single minute, while 105 people die each minute.

'Population stabilisation should become a priority for sustainable development.'

Kofi Annan, United Nations (UN) Secretary-General 1997–2006

YOUR PLANET NEEDS YOU

This discussion has to be a broad one. It may touch upon science, economics, politics and ethics. Let's look at all these issues and see how we can work together as humans and as part of one living planet.

EMPTY WILDERNESS

While many people cram into cities to live, large parts of the world, such as Mongolia (below), are almost deserted. Conditions in these places are either too harsh for people to live in or they are too remote and cut off from the rest of the world.

In 1950, just 30 per cent of the world's population lived in cities. Today, more than half the world's population live in urban areas. By 2050, this will grow to two-thirds.

The world's population is getting bigger. In many parts of the world overcrowding is an issue and resources are limited. In each chapter of this book we'll look at different aspects of the topic of population, exploring and discussing the issues involved. There are vital questions to be raised and discussed.

Let's talk about them.

SEVEN BILLION
AND COUNTING

News headlines often talk of a population 'explosion'. You can see why. In 1800, the world population was about 1 billion. By 1960, it was 3 billion. Today, the total is about 7.4 billion. To put that in perspective, it means that about seven per cent of all the people who have ever lived are alive today. A baby is born somewhere in the world every 3.4 seconds.

AN ANCIENT WORRY

The fear of a population explosion has been around for at least 2,500 years. More than 1,700 years ago, when the world population was only about 190 million, a North African writer called Tertullian was already talking about the planet being unable to support so many people.

THE BLACK DEATH
This picture shows the horror of the Black Death, which caused the deaths of between 85 and 300 million people.

UPS AND DOWNS

Falls in population were also a great worry in ancient times. Population levels crash when there is war, famine or disease, or when many people die in childbirth. The Black Death ravaged Asia and Europe in the 1340s and '50s. Today, people can expect to live longer when there is food, prosperity, peace, medicine and healthcare.

NUMBER CRUNCH

The global birth rate is about 18.6 live births per 1,000 population in a year.

Large-scale immunisation has protected millions of people from illness and even wiped out some diseases, such as smallpox, from the planet.

FUTURE TRENDS

Today, the world's population growth rate is about 1.13 per cent. That has fallen from a 1970s high of 2.1 per cent. So on a global scale, growth is falling. But that still means huge increases because the population base is still bigger than before. The UN has forecast a total population of 9.7 billion by 2050 and approximately 11.2 billion by 2100. The numbers are then expected to peak and stabilise (see pages 8–9). But there are still many unknown factors, such as the effects of climate change.

HOW MANY PEOPLE?

The study of population statistics is called demography. How many people are there and where do they live? An official count is called a census. The earliest known census took place in Babylon over 6,000 years ago. Its purpose was to work out how much food was needed by the population. Today, most governments carry out a census every ten years or so.

POPULATION INFORMATION

The 2011 census in India registered 1,210,854,977 people, an increase of 17.7 per cent since 2001. A modern census does much more than count heads. It often asks people all sorts of questions about their age, gender, housing, literacy, ethnic group, language or work. Some people complain that governments ask too many questions that are none of their business. But all this information can be useful for efficient social and economic planning, for building new hospitals, schools, houses, roads or factories.

NUMBER CRUNCH

In 2017, China had an estimated population of 1,388,233,000.

By 2022, India is expected to overtake China as the world's most populous country.

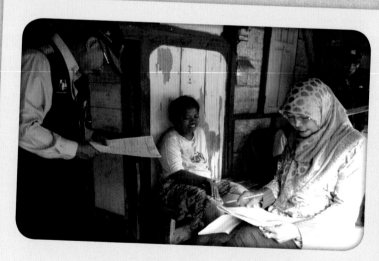

COUNTING HEADS

Census taking, such as here in Indonesia, can involve thousands of data collectors going from house to house to gather the information.

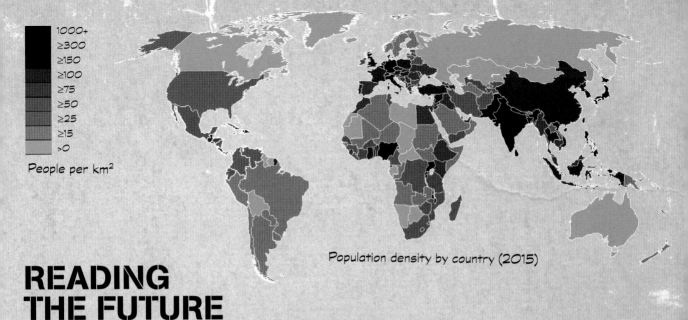

Population density by country (2015)

READING THE FUTURE

Censuses and other sources such as public health statistics can provide the data for mathematical modelling. Computers are used to work out possibilities for future population dynamics, such as growth rates, peaks and declines. Economics or environmental changes may need to be factored into the calculations. By seeing the population densities of different regions and countries (above), politicians and agencies can work out which parts of the world need more or less resources.

GROWING WORLD POPULATION

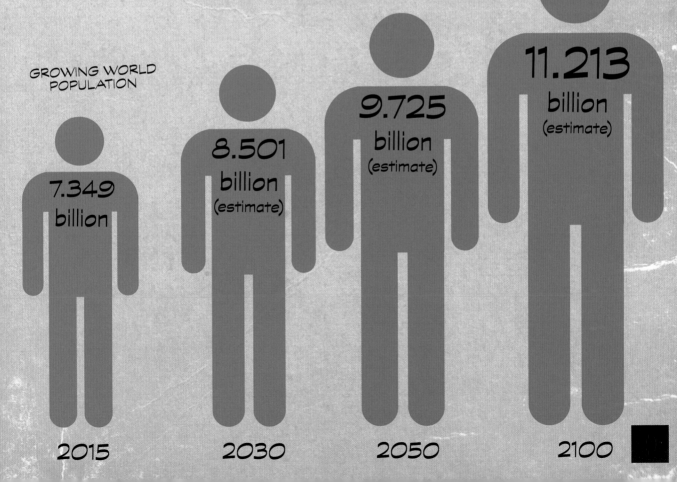

7.349 billion

8.501 billion (estimate)

9.725 billion (estimate)

11.213 billion (estimate)

2015

2030

2050

2100

WHO, WHERE, WHEN?

Is it all about numbers? If so, how can we judge if the estimates of future population increases are correct? Well, the UN says we can be about 95 per cent sure that the world total for 2030 will be between 8.4 and 8.6 billion, and for 2100 somewhere between 9.5 and 13.3 billion. Birth rates are still high and the odds of the population levelling off or falling before the end of this century are about 23 per cent.

FEWER BABIES

The big picture only begins to make sense when we look at it in more detail. In Asia, which today has by far the biggest share of the world's population, the number of babies per mother is already beginning to fall. In the developed countries of Europe, people are living to an older age. With fewer younger people having babies, Europe's populations are set to shrink, although immigration could boost the numbers.

City planners overcome the problem of increasing populations by building densely packed high-rise accommodation, such as these towers in Hong Kong.

EDUCATION
A good standard of education can play a key role in reducing population growth rates, as children learn more about the outside world and jobs and opportunities instead of worrying about life at home.

FUTURE FERTILITY
In the world as a whole, today's average of 2.5 children per mother is expected to drop to 2 by the end of this century. The biggest population growth in coming years will be in Africa, which has the most young people and, because of a lower life expectancy, the fewest old people. However, even here the fertility rate is expected to drop from 4.7 to 2.2 children per woman by 2100.

NUMBER CRUNCH
How is the population spread around the world?

NORTH AMERICA
363 million
24.49 million km²

WORLD
7.5 billion
510.1 million km²

EUROPE
743 million
10.18 million km²

ASIA
4.5 billion
43.82 million km²

AFRICA
1.3 billion
30.37 million km²

SOUTH AMERICA
(including Caribbean)
648 million
17.84 million km²

Population
(est 2017)
Land area km²

OCEANIA
41 million
8.5 million km²

LET'S DISCUSS...
THE BIRTH RATE MAY BE AFFECTED BY

- better nutrition.
- education levels.
- lack of poverty.
- empowerment of women.

- disease.
- war and conflict.
- famine.

1 FACES IN THE CROWD

HUMANS

Mapping population by nations and numbers doesn't really tell the whole story. Countries are more than colours on a map. The natural world has no borders other than rivers, coastlines or mountain ranges. The borders on maps have been invented by nations and empires. Often they bear little relation to the cultures, languages and histories of the population.

Arctic peoples live in northern Canada, Greenland, the USA and Russia.

WHO ARE WE?

A global population of 7 billion means 7 billion individuals. These fit into all kinds of interactive social networks. People may identify themselves in relation to an ethnic group, a region, a language, a religion, or by their political or social institutions or their income. Populations may be mapped according to any of these categories.

People living in the USA come from a wide range of ethnic backgrounds.

ONE RACE, THE HUMAN RACE

Traditionally, human populations have been categorised by appearance, such as their skin colour, their features, or notions of 'race'. Appearance may well suggest a person's ancestors. However, race is not a clear enough category to be of much scientific use, because there are genetic differences within each grouping and genetic similarities across the groupings. Differences are minimal: ultimately, we all have the same ancestors.

Brazil is famous for its huge festivals, celebrated by its mix of European and indigenous cultures.

A MELTING POT

Racism emphasises difference and attempts to set up one group of humans as superior to another. It is based on political or social prejudice rather than science. Peoples and cultures have always interacted and mixed. This process has been hastened over the ages by global empires, by trade and by the movement of peoples.

LET'S DISCUSS...
CULTURAL DIFFERENCES IN POPULATION

- enrich all our cultures.
- increase our understanding of humanity.
- offer chances for cooperation.

- may result in conflict.
- may be exploited by racists.
- may hinder cooperation.

These Swedish people are celebrating the festival of Saint Lucy's Day.

These two Temuan boys are part of an indigenous group of people who live in Malaysia.

This group of children live in Papua New Guinea.

A Berber boy looking after his herd of goats. The Berber people live in northern Africa.

ON THE MOVE

We tend to think of population in terms of settled communities, but humans have been on the move around the planet ever since they first evolved as a species in Africa. As hunters they followed their prey from one hunting ground to another. Only with the invention of farming could they settle in one place, building villages and towns. But herders and traders often kept up a nomadic way of life, and some still do today.

EMIGRATION, IMMIGRATION

Many people today choose to move, to live and work in another country. Immigration can increase the workforce and bring new skills. Emigration can leave a country depopulated. Economic life has become globalised, and large firms are now transnational, producing and selling goods in many different countries. The Internet and modern transport have helped the world to shrink.

These refugees are living in a makeshift camp in Somalia. Many people fled the country when its government collapsed in 1991, leading to a vicious civil war.

NUMBER CRUNCH

In 2015, over a million migrants and refugees entered countries of the European Union (EU).

WORKING MIGRANTS

Some migrants move to meet the demands of seasonal labour. These people on a strawberry farm in the UK have travelled from Poland to work through the fruit-picking season.

REFUGEES

Throughout history great movements of people have been triggered by natural disasters, famine or war. The victims have no choice but to seek refuge or asylum in another land. During the Second World War (1939–1945), many millions of Europeans were displaced. In 1950, the new United Nations founded an agency to help refugees, which became the United Nations High Commissioner for Refugees (UNHCR). In 2016, it reported that 65.3 million people were now displaced, nearly one per cent of the world's population. Much of this was the result of wars in Afghanistan, Iraq, Syria, South Sudan, the Horn of Africa and Libya. Refugees fleeing war and natural disasters, such as drought, have found themselves exploited by people traffickers. Many people have drowned in small boats while trying to reach safety in countries such as Greece or Italy.

LET'S DISCUSS...
REFUGEES FROM WAR

- could seek asylum abroad even in the ancient world.

- have a right to asylum under modern international law.

- deserve our help — we could all find ourselves in their situation.

- have no choice but to flee their homes.

- often risk their lives to escape.

- often become separated from their families.

15

RESPONSES TO MIGRATION

Migration is a key issue in debates about population. The USA as a nation was created by refugees and economic migrants. Yet today there is talk of raising walls and closing borders. While some migrants are welcomed and helped, others are met with fear or abuse.

REFUGEES FROM WAR

may have no choice but to flee their homes and to save the lives of their families. We have a moral duty to help them and welcome them.

NUMBER CRUNCH

Since 2011, the war in Syria has had a catastrophic impact.

- Displaced people inside Syria numbered 6.6 million

THE SITUATION MAY BE JUST

as bad for those refugees fleeing persecution because of their politics, their religion or their sexuality.

IF PEOPLE WANT TO STOP OTHERS

from becoming refugees or migrants, they should stop the bombing of their countries and work to eradicate global poverty and injustice.

- Approximate number of Syrian refugees elsewhere:

  - Turkey 2.7 million
  - Lebanon 1.1 million
  - Jordan 657,000
  - Germany 429,000
  - Saudi Arabia 500,000

QUESTION IT!
SHOULD COUNTRIES WELCOME REFUGEES AND MIGRANTS?

DO BORDERS NEED BETTER CONTROLS? Might some refugees pose a security risk?

ARE WARS IN DISTANT lands the concern of all of us? Do economic migrants deserve the same rights as refugees from war?

SOME SAY THAT if you let in a few migrants, more and more will want to come, placing a strain on services such as schools, employment, housing and healthcare.

2 CITY BOOM

Another great shift of population is taking place within national borders. People are moving into towns and cities. This process is called urbanisation and is increasing at the rate of two per cent per year. Urbanisation really took off at the start of the Industrial Revolution, in the 1800s. In our own times it is racing ahead. Fifty-four per cent of the world's people now live in cities.

BIG SPRAWL

In 1979, Shenzhen in China had a population of 30,000. Today, its population numbers 10.8 million and it is part of a vast urban sprawl covering the Pearl River delta. Cities merge with each other to form huge megacities, with more than 10 million people. Today, Tokyo, the capital of Japan, is home to over 38 million people.

MIGRANT LABOURERS
In China, many people have moved from rural areas and villages to the country's growing cities where they can find work on construction sites.

MONEY DREAMS

People leave the countryside in search of work and an easier life. Huge numbers of people in China have moved into cities over the last 25 years, sending whatever money they make back to their families in the countryside. After a downturn in the economy in 2015, many went home again. In many parts of the world, from Africa to South America, the incomers neither make money nor return home. They live in makeshift slums known as favelas or shantytowns, often without clean water, proper sanitation or power.

Manila

NUMBER CRUNCH
At least eight of the world's cities now have a population of more than 20 million. Many cities are desperately overcrowded. The city district of Manila, in the Philippines, has 41,515 people per km² while the whole of Mongolia has a density of less than two per km².

Moscow's business centre (below) is a symbol of the economic power of the Russian capital. In contrast, whole towns and villages in the countryside have been abandoned (right).

ABANDONED!

The countryside left behind by urbanisation may become depopulated. In recent years so many Russians have moved to the capital, Moscow, that they have left behind 'ghost villages' without schools or services. History warns us that cities too can die. The world has many abandoned cities, lost in the sand or covered by jungle. Cities cannot grow indefinitely. They must be in the right place at the right time, with enough trade and resources. Even today's megacities must be sustainable if they are to survive.

LET'S DISCUSS...
BIG CITIES

- drive the economy.
- are often centres of government.
- house millions of people.

- use up resources.
- pollute the air.
- become overcrowded.

NATURE UNDER PRESSURE

Big cities eat up the countryside as they grow. The natural world around them is a complex network of plant and animal species that interact with each other. Humans are part of these ecosystems, but we do not seem to realise that we are poisoning or destroying the very resources that sustain us. Does the rise in population pose a threat to the natural world? Are humans the most dangerous animals on the planet?

SPACE INVADERS

At the moment, about 95 per cent of the world's population lives on just 10 per cent of the land surface. Large areas of the remainder are taken up by farmland or road and rail networks. Yes, there is enough physical space for the population to expand. The problem is that when human settlement expands outwards into grassland, woodland or forest, it fragments the natural habitat.

DUST BOWL

During the 1930s, severe drought and poor farming techniques on the US prairies destroyed the topsoil, turning it into dust that was blown away. This created huge dust storms that buried whole farms.

FACTORY SHIPS

Super-sized factory ships (left) use the latest radar technology and massive nets to catch enormous amounts of fish, depleting stocks to the extent that they cannot recover.

TOO MUCH IMPACT

Growing populations are greedy for resources. Rainforest, the richest type of environment on the planet, is cut down for crops or for ranching. New roads let in settlers, hunters and illegal miners. Humans are often bad neighbours. The current extinction rate of other species is now at least a thousand times the normal or 'background' rate. Nearly all of that increase is because of human activities.

TIME FOR CHANGE

Fortunately humans do know how to conserve and protect species, how to stop forests being stripped bare, how to farm sustainably and still feed the populations projected for the future. But if we are to fit a growing population into the environment, we have to change the way we do things and make sure that protection of the environment is enforced by law.

Expansion of cities has brought them into conflict with plants and animals, threatening food sources and the amount of space they can live in. This giraffe is living within sight of Nairobi, Kenya.

LET'S DISCUSS...
POPULATION INCREASE MEANS THAT

- we need to share resources more carefully.
- we need to protect the environment.
- we need to change the way we use land.

- we create more pollution.
- we fragment natural habitats.
- we threaten other species.

LIVING IN THE GREENHOUSE

Humans need breathing space, but today over 7 billion people own 1.2 billion cars. Along congested city roads their exhaust fumes often form a toxic, chemical smog that hangs in the air. Many power stations and factories also still burn fossil fuels such as oil, gas and coal, which give out large amounts of carbon dioxide (CO_2). At the moment governments around the world are desperately trying to reduce these carbon emissions.

WARMING WORLD

Global warming could lead to more extreme weather events, such as powerful storms and flooding, as experienced by these people in Bangladesh.

CAR-MAGEDDON

The Brazilian city of São Paulo has some of the worst traffic jams on the planet, with tailbacks stretching up to 295 km on a very bad day.

CARBON OVERLOAD

Most scientists blame the emissions for changing the climate, warming the land surface and the oceans. Normally, CO_2 is soaked up by the oceans and forests on Earth. Now it seems excessive amounts of this and other 'greenhouse gases' are becoming trapped in the atmosphere and reflecting radiation back to Earth. Global warming is already happening, and it is estimated that by 2100 the average global temperature could have increased by between 1.8°C and 4°C – with disastrous consequences.

POPULATION AND CLIMATE CHANGE

The effects of climate change might include rising sea levels, extreme tropical storms, drought, flooding, acidification of the oceans and more species extinctions. If the human population is growing so fast, it couldn't be doing it at a worse time. Of course, population growth and the severe effects of industrialisation have taken place over much of the same time period. They are part of the same process.

LET'S DISCUSS... THE EFFECTS OF CLIMATE CHANGE

- can be reduced by clean energy and clean transport.
- can be reduced by planting new forests.
- can be reduced by saving energy and cutting waste.

- cannot be reversed quickly.
- may threaten food supplies for a larger population.
- may be made worse by population increase.

Recent international agreements have tried to limit the levels of emissions, such as those from this factory in Siberia, Russia. So far, these agreements have had limited success.

23

BIGGER AND BIGGER

Population increase is often discussed in general terms. What does it mean at the practical level? Infrastructure is the word we use to describe the basic services that allow a society to function, the roads, power lines, schools and hospitals. Will we be able to pay for what will be needed?

QUESTION IT!

CAN THE WORLD COPE WITH A BIGGER POPULATION?

THERE IS ENOUGH room in the world for expansion, if environmental problems can be managed.

POPULATION INCREASE as a result of urbanisation can in theory improve infrastructure, as in a densely populated district people can access services more easily than in the remote countryside.

THERE ARE TECHNICAL solutions to some of the infrastructure problems created by bigger populations. For example, low-carbon and recycled building materials can be used to provide cheap housing. Small-scale renewable energy can be provided for a low cost at a community level.

IF WE WANT to keep population numbers down, research shows that the most important way of reducing the fertility rate is to make sure that young women receive an education and more opportunities in life.

POPULATION INCREASE

will have a global impact, but it will be felt the hardest in the world's least developed regions, which are already struggling to maintain infrastructure.

THE RISE IN NUMBERS

of young people across a region means that more and more need placing in schools. Class sizes are a problem. In southern Africa, for example, to achieve one teacher per class of 40 at primary level and one per 35 at secondary level would need the building of about 50,000 new classrooms.

ADEQUATE FUNDING

for increased provision of education, healthcare and other social services is just not there in the least developed regions of the world, even though these are the very ways in which population growth will be reduced.

WATER AND WELLS

Water is the key to life on Earth. Humans need to drink about two litres of the precious liquid every day. We also use it for washing, cleaning, cooking, sanitation, manufacture, irrigating crops and watering livestock. Most of us have water piped to our homes from reservoirs, but in many parts of the world people still have to access water from wells.

NUMBER CRUNCH

7.4 billion – world population 2016

2.8 billion people worldwide suffer some water shortage.

1.2 billion lack access to clean drinking water.

2.5 billion lack access to proper sanitation.

THIRSTY WORK

Fresh water withdrawals have tripled over the last 50 years, while the amount of available water has dwindled. There are already water shortages in many parts of the world. Pressure comes from population growth, which increases water demand by about 64 billion m^3 every year. Urbanisation makes matters worse. Some large cities barely have enough water to supply people, let alone thirsty industries. Irrigation of crops may be crucial in providing food for ever more hungry mouths.

A WARMER WORLD

The future dangers of climate change (see pages 22–23) may contain unknown factors, but will certainly affect water supplies in many ways. Droughts and desertification may increase. Rising sea levels may flood coastal aquifers with undrinkable salty water.

SAVE IT!

Water management on a large scale is needed to cut out waste and ensure that aquifers are sustainable. Desalination – the removal of salt from sea water – is an expensive industrial process, but is improving all the time. Small units for the home or the village can distill salty or dirty water to make it drinkable.

COMMUNAL PUMPS

These children on the Philippine island of Luzon are washing clothes with water from a communal pump. Access to clean water is a big problem in the Philippines, where only five per cent of households are connected to a mains sewer.

VILLAGE WELL

Two young boys pump water from a well in a village in India. Water shortages have always been acute in India, but in recent years there has been a big push to connect more rural homes to piped water and to increase the time during which water is available.

A drought has caused the earth to crack in the wilderness of British Columbia, Canada. Drought not only means less water for people to drink, it can also damage crops, leaving less food for people to eat.

LET'S DISCUSS...
WATER SUPPLIES

- are threatened by population increase.
- are threatened by waste.
- are threatened by climate change.

- ensure human survival.
- are endlessly replenished by rainfall.
- need to be clean and healthy.

ENOUGH TO EAT

English cleric Thomas Robert Malthus (1766–1834) believed that hopes for a better world were put at risk by a constant race between food production and population growth. Many of his views are disputed today, but he did challenge the common view at the time that population growth was always a good thing.

HUNGER

Today, we seem to be in a situation where population growth is running ahead of food production, yet again. It is estimated that about 795 million people are short of food. In the developing regions of the world around 13 per cent of the population are undernourished, and over three million children a year die of malnutrition.

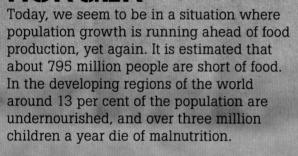

GROWING MORE FOOD

The UN's Food and Agriculture Organisation (FAO) reckons that if the world's population passes the 9.1 billion mark by 2050, world food production will need to increase by about 70 per cent. With climate change threatening crops, that's quite a scary prospect, even with more drought-resistant strains of plants.

KEEP IT SMALL

In some parts of the world where growing conditions are harsh, such as Ethiopia, small farms are better suited to the environment than large-scale industrialised versions.

CAN IT BE BETTER?

But it's not all about growing more. Perhaps we could be growing and distributing our food in a more rational way. Does it make sense for farmers in the tropics to stop growing food for their communities and replace these with cash crops for export, as many are doing now? Does it make sense to raise beef cattle when soya produces far more protein per hectare, and more cheaply? It has been said that the amount of grain used to feed all the cattle in the USA could sustain 800 million people instead. Farming has become a global business with food traded as an industrial commodity. Some say things are more efficient that way, others that it turns food production into a lottery, as prices rise and fall on the market.

NUMBER CRUNCH

According to the FAO about 1.3 billion tonnes of food each year is simply wasted or lost. That's about one-third of all the food produced.

LET'S DISCUSS...
FOOD SUPPLY

Many cattle in Brazil graze on land that has been cleared of its natural rainforest.

• could be improved by cutting food waste.

• could be improved by hardier, drought-resistant crops.

• could be improved by focusing more on local farming than on export crops.

• is suffering from decreasing water resources.

• is disrupted by war and international conflict.

• is often at risk from the effects of climate change.

RICH WORLD, POOR WORLD

What do we mean when we say someone is poor? Poverty can be defined as lacking the money or means to obtain life's basic necessities, such as food. According to the World Bank's 2015–2016 survey, 9.6 per cent of the world's population currently live on less than 1.90 US dollars a day. Poverty can also mean being deprived of a home, healthcare, a clean water supply, education or security.

THE GAP

Poverty is found in all countries, but is at its most extreme in the world's least developed regions. The World Bank claims poverty has been decreasing in recent years, although it is very hard to measure accurately. The gap between rich and poor has actually been growing in many countries. The world's most developed nations may have only 13 per cent of the world's population, but they have 45 per cent of its purchasing power. There is inequality within the developed nations, too, with the richest 10 per cent of the population making nearly ten times as much money as the poorest 10 per cent.

TEMPORARY SHELTER
Without a permanent roof over their heads, many poor people live in makeshift shelters, such as these tents in Paris, France.

A LIFE IN POVERTY
Poverty can affect all aspects of a child's life, from the quality of the food they eat to their access to education and healthcare.

POVERTY AND POPULATION GROWTH

There is a moral duty to tackle poverty, as well as an obvious economic case. Different political systems may try to deal with the issue in different ways. Poverty in the least developed regions is linked with young populations and a high fertility rate (see pages 10–11). If life expectancy is low, then having more children may seem to be a way of securing the future and increasing family income.

'Poverty is the worst form of violence.'
Mohandas K (Mahatma) Gandhi,
Indian activist (1869–1948)

A homeless woman begs for money in the street in the Italian city of Verona.

LET'S DISCUSS...
GLOBAL POVERTY

- eradication is a top target of the United Nations.
- has been reduced in recent years.
- must be tackled alongside inequality.

- encourages high population growth.
- holds back social development.
- may be made worse by the effects of climate change.

GLOBAL TRADE

Globalisation is the reorganisation of business and trade to operate transnationally – across national borders. It is based on capitalist or 'free-market' economics and it shapes the lives of us all. But does it reduce poverty or increase it?

QUESTION IT!
DOES GLOBALISATION HELP GET RID OF POVERTY?

SUPPORTERS OF GLOBALISATION say that it creates wealth and employment and brings down prices.

A THRIVING ECONOMY may help the poor either directly or indirectly. It is more likely to create a climate for democratic government, in which the poor have their own voice.

FAIRTRADE

Some organisations, such as the Fairtrade Foundation, campaign for better trade agreements between rich countries and suppliers from poorer nations. Companies that meet the Fairtrade conditions are allowed to carry a Fairtrade symbol on their packaging.

These coffee farmers from Uganda are guaranteed a fair price for their crop under a Fairtrade scheme.

GLOBALISATION BRINGS FOREIGN INVESTMENT and the latest technology, which a less developed nation would be unable to afford on its own. It encourages modern communication and transport, and the development of infrastructure.

A child works in a car repair centre in the Indian city of Kolkata. According to statistics given by the Indian government there are 20 million child workers in the country.

AN EXAMPLE OF GLOBALISATION'S FAILURE is ongoing inequality. The wealthiest 20 per cent of the world's population consumes 86 per cent of the resources.

MANY TRANSNATIONAL CORPORATIONS are richer and even more powerful than national governments. They are not accountable to anyone except their shareholders.

'Trade justice for the developing world and for this generation is a truly significant way for the developed countries to show commitment to bringing about an end to global poverty.'

Nelson Mandela (1918–2013), President of South Africa 1994–1999

GLOBALISATION IS NOT A PARTNERSHIP of equals. Small local companies find it hard to compete with the giants.

33

4 POPULATION PLANNING

The birth of a child is an important and exciting event. Education about family planning plays a very important part in making sure that childbirth is successful for all concerned. Women and men can plan carefully whether they want children and, if so, how many they are going to have and when.

BIRTH CONTROL

In society as a whole, family planning can play a crucial role in controlling the birth rate. Contraception is the prevention of conception, either by taking a pill or by using a barrier such as a condom during intercourse. A condom can also protect against the spread of sexually transmitted diseases, such as HIV. The need for contraception can be permanently removed by sterilisation or by vasectomy. Some religious groups oppose birth control, but even within the same religions there may be different beliefs and policies.

为了国家富强家庭幸

福请您实行计划生育

塘山乡人民政府宣

FAMILY PLANNING
This government sign tells Chinese people 'For a prosperous, powerful and a happy family, please practise family planning'.

FAMILY PLANNING PROGRAMMES

The Indian government was the first to encourage family planning as a means of stabilising population growth, in 1952. Today, birth control is supported by the UN and by the World Health Organisation. Contraception empowers women in society. It reduces the number of unwanted or dangerous births and abortions (the ending of unwanted pregnancies).

A Chinese family with one child walk through the streets of the capital city, Beijing.

LET'S DISCUSS...
CONTRACEPTION

- was used by only 33 per cent of couples in Africa in 2015, compared with 75 per cent in North America.
- was an unmet need for 12 per cent of women worldwide in 2015.
- will remain an unmet need for many couples in 2030.

- was used worldwide by 64 per cent of couples in 2015.
- is expected to increase in areas of high population growth.
- use is expected to rise by 20 million couples by 2030.

A ONE-CHILD POLICY

From 1979, the Chinese government, which was worried about population numbers, brought in a law requiring many parents to have just one child. The fact that they were given no choice was seen as a breach of human rights and attracted international criticism. As from 2016, China has had a two-child limit.

GOOD BREEDING OR BAD?

Some ancient religious texts call for people to have as many children as possible. These were mostly written at a time when the global population was very small, but some people still respect these doctrines. However, the will to stabilise population growth in the future interests of humanity and the planet can also be seen as healthy, life affirming and necessary for our times.

EARLY SUPPORT
English statistician Sir Francis Galton (1822–1911) was the first person to use the term 'eugenics'.

WHAT IS EUGENICS?

In the 1800s, there was new scientific understanding about heredity. Farmers found ways of 'improving' their animals through selective breeding, making a priority of 'useful' characteristics. People read the work of Charles Darwin (1809–1882) about natural selection in the evolution of species. By the 1900s, the idea became very widespread that human populations could be 'improved', by encouraging the reproduction of certain groups of people more than others. This was called eugenics.

'The great problem of civilisation is to secure a relative increase of the valuable as compared with the less valuable or noxious elements in the population.'

US President Theodore Roosevelt, 1913

THE ROAD TO AUSCHWITZ

The supporters of eugenics by definition place greater value on some human groups or characteristics than on others. Should the ability to have children be dependent on the supposed intelligence, social class, criminal record or race of the parents? The danger of these ideas became all too clear under Nazi rule in Germany in the 1930s and '40s. The Jews, Roma, homosexuals, and other people whom the Nazis claimed were 'inferior' were first banned from marrying Germans, and then murdered in their millions in death camps, such as Auschwitz in Poland. Disabled people too were sterilised or killed.

NAZI CHILDREN
These babies are being cared for at a special Nazi hospital built to promote the birth of children who had been born to racially 'pure' parents.

Railway tracks lead to the gates of Auschwitz, a concentration camp in Poland, where some 1.1 million people were killed by the Nazis.

LET'S DISCUSS...
POPULATION CONTROL

• must always be voluntary.

• must always be in the interests of the individual.

• can benefit the future of humanity.

• must never be forced upon the individual.

• must never favour one social or ethnic group above another.

• can lead at its most extreme to injustice or murder.

ABORTION

Reproductive rights are about a person's right to family planning advice, contraception, abortion, sex education and healthcare. They raise key questions about population control, which may be debated from ethical or religious points of view. Abortion has taken place throughout history, but the social attitudes towards it have varied according to time and place.

ABORTION IS GENERALLY A SAFE operation when conducted legally by qualified doctors at an early stage in the pregnancy. Where abortions are illegal, they may cause injury, infection or even the death of the mother.

IT IS A WOMAN'S MORAL RIGHT to choose freely what to do with her body. She should have the right not to give birth, just as she should have the right to give birth if she wants to. It is rarely a choice taken without grave consideration.

ABORTION MAY MEAN that a woman does not have to bear the child of someone who has raped her. In some cases an abortion may be needed to save the life of the mother.

IN ITS EARLY STAGES, a foetus is unable to exist independently outside the womb. Until then, it is regarded by many doctors as still being a part of the mother's body. In the UK, an abortion is permitted in most cases up to 24 weeks after conception, provided two doctors agree that abortion is best for the mother's physical or mental health. In cases of severe risk to the mother's health, or medical problems with the foetus, abortion may take place after 24 weeks.

'You cannot have maternal health without reproductive health. And reproductive health includes contraception and family planning and access to legal, safe abortion.'

Hillary Clinton (1947–),
67th US Secretary of State, 2010

QUESTION IT!
IS THERE A CASE FOR LEGAL ABORTION?

UNWANTED CHILDREN can always be adopted.

ABORTION CAN BE USED AS JUST ANOTHER MEANS OF CONTRACEPTION. And in some countries, it is often used to terminate a foetus solely on the grounds of gender, because boy babies are preferred.

OPPONENTS OF ABORTION argue that the right to life of an unborn child is the same as for any human being. Terminating this life is a form of murder.

ABORTION MAY LEAD TO LATER birth complications or disease.

Some people are opposed to abortion on religious grounds. These people holding crosses are taking part in an anti-abortion demonstration in Munich, Germany, in 2014.

A BRAVE NEW WORLD?

Genetics is one area of science which may have a big effect on population and even make people question what it means to be human. Genes, which are made of a chemical called DNA, pass on programming for life from parents to children. We each have about 20,000 genes and these can carry hereditary disease alongside all the useful information.

NEW GENES FOR OLD

If doctors could replace 'bad' genes with 'good' genes, hereditary disease might be prevented or cured. Scientists are trying to make this gene therapy work. A few experiments seem promising, treating cancers or problems with the immune system. However there are many ethical concerns. Some people might want to choose which genes their future children might have. That may never be possible, and trying to do it may cause damage. It also raises ethical questions. Do we as a society really want rich people to buy even more advantages for their children?

This image shows the twisted strands of a DNA molecule. Between the two strands are bridges and the order of these bridges determines the genetic make-up of a person.

GOOD DREAMS AND BAD DREAMS

Will scientists ever be able to reproduce whole humans by cloning? Cloning has already been achieved with other animals, such as sheep. Could this be done with humans? Genetic research opens up all sorts of opportunities but also plenty of traps. Will genetic engineering give some people too much power? In 1934, Aldous Huxley (1894–1963) wrote a novel called *Brave New World*. In it he imagined a future world where natural reproduction is no longer allowed. Human embryos are grown in hatcheries. The lowest social classes are cloned, and all except the upper classes are treated with chemicals to give them lower intelligence. Will that future ever be possible, or is it just a nightmare, written as a warning?

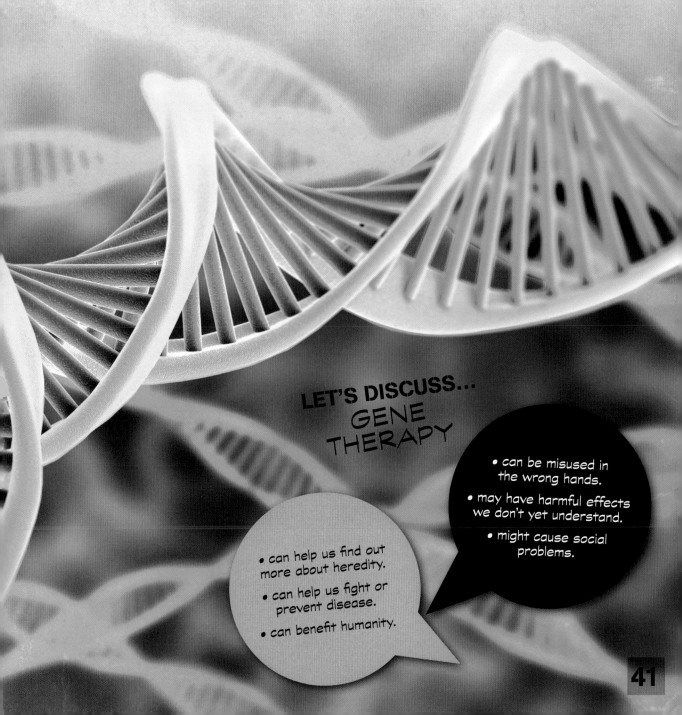

LET'S DISCUSS...
GENE THERAPY

- can be misused in the wrong hands.
- may have harmful effects we don't yet understand.
- might cause social problems.

- can help us find out more about heredity.
- can help us fight or prevent disease.
- can benefit humanity.

PEOPLE TOGETHER

The big population rise over the next 100 years cannot be avoided. Numbers are certain to continue on a steep upwards curve. The data suggest that they will peak and then level off early in the next century. We have seen how population increase cannot be viewed in isolation, as just a game of numbers.

The poor in many cities have to live in cramped housing, such as this favela in Rio de Janeiro, Brazil.

LIVING SPACE
The world's richest people can afford to live in homes with all the facilities they could want and plenty of surrounding space. This home is in Tuscany, Italy.

COMPLEX PROBLEMS

Population increase is one strand in a complicated knot of related issues. These include climate change, the environment, global economics and poverty, politics, conflict and war, migration, sustainable resources, farming and food, new science and technology, population controls and genetics. The task ahead is immense. There is no simple trick that can solve it easily and quickly. It will need careful unpicking over a long time, with patience and determination.

WAYS FORWARD

Never before have humans had a better understanding of demography, climate science and the many other areas that need action. What they are not so good at is cooperating with each other. Even in this globalised world, progress is held back by endless warfare. We don't want to control population in the medieval way, by mass death and famine. We need to do it by respecting human rights. Human rights are at the heart of all population issues, from migration to eradicating poverty and improving access to education. Population means human beings.

LET'S DISCUSS...
POPULATION PRIORITIES

- include tackling poverty and inequality.
- include improving education.
- include giving more political power to young women.

- may be hindered by international conflicts.
- may be made harder by climate change.
- cannot be solved by division.

5 UNIVERSAL RIGHTS

On 10 December 1948 the United Nations General Assembly adopted a Universal Declaration of Human Rights. After the terrible tragedy of the Second World War, this was the first attempt to set out a positive plan for the freedom and wellbeing of everyone in the world. Human rights are an essential part of dealing effectively with the world's population crisis.

QUESTION IT!
SHOULD THE SAME HUMAN RIGHTS APPLY TO EVERY SINGLE PERSON IN THE WORLD?

SURELY 'UNIVERSAL' means these rights should apply to everyone – provided these do not run against the spirit of the declaration?

THE DECLARATION supports equality and it should apply to all people, regardless of who they are. It supports the right to life, liberty and social security, the freedom of movement, the right to asylum, the right to marry freely and to raise a family, and the right to work.

ALL THESE RIGHTS need to be honoured if the world is to function efficiently and fairly, and if population levels are to stabilise.

SOME PEOPLE might say that although the principles of the declaration are good, they are little more than fine words. But the declaration has become a part of many international treaties. They are targets rather than laws, and they really are worth meeting.

'To deny people their human rights is to challenge their very humanity.'

Nelson Mandela, 1990

SOME PEOPLE say that sections of the declaration are not compatible with their own religion, which to them has more authority. Some say that the declaration goes against their local social or cultural traditions, so it is exclusive rather than inclusive.

People from poorer countries, such as these children from Niger, don't always enjoy the same rights as people living in richer countries, such as the right to live in safety and to have a education.

SOME CRITICS SAY that the wording in places begs further questions or definitions. For example, a right to life can mean different things to different people, as in debates about abortion.

45

GLOSSARY

ACIDIFICATION
An increase in the levels of acid in a substance, such as sea water.

ASYLUM SEEKER
Somebody who seeks refuge from war or persecution in another country.

BIRTH RATE
The proportion of live births to total population within a particular location and time frame, such as per 1,000 people per year.

CAPITALISM
An economic system based on private ownership, profit and competition.

CASH CROP
Crops that are grown commercially, rather than for local use by the farmer or the community.

CENSUS
An official population count and gathering of information about the people.

CIVIL WAR
A war between groups in the same country.

CLIMATE CHANGE
A change in the long-term weather conditions on Earth.

CLONING
The artificial replication of cells and tissues to create an identical living being.

CONTRACEPTION
Preventing conception, often by the use of a chemical or a barrier such as a condom.

CONURBATION
The joining together of separate towns or cities as they expand.

DISPLACED
Forced to move from one's home or country because of war or a natural disaster.

DNA
Deoxyribonucleic acid, a substance that makes up the genes which programme life and heredity.

ECONOMIC MIGRANTS
People who move to another country to escape poverty or seek work.

ECOSYSTEM
An interactive network of living things within their environment.

EMIGRATION
Moving from one's own country to live in another.

ETHICAL
Guided by moral principles, having a sense of what is right or wrong.

ETHNIC GROUP
A community of people who share a common descent or culture.

EUGENICS
A belief that the genetic quality of the human population needs 'improvement' by selective breeding.

EVOLVE
The gradual change in the form of living organisms as they adapt to the environment in which they live.

EXTINCTION
The dying out and disappearance of a living species.

FAMILY PLANNING
Enabling individuals to choose how many children they have and when, and how to achieve this.

FERTILITY RATE
The number of live births to women within a location, often expressed per 1,000 per year.

FOETUS
A baby as it develops in the womb, before being born.

FREE MARKET
A system of trade that is based on market values with little government regulation.

GENETICS
The scientific study of genes and how traits are passed on from one generation to the next.

GLOBALISATION
The creation of a world economy based on corporations and agreements rather than nations.

HORN OF AFRICA
The horn-shaped part of eastern Africa, which sticks out into the Indian Ocean.

IMMIGRATION
The movement of people into a country or a region in search of work or somewhere to live.

IMMUNISATION
Protecting people from disease, often by injecting them with a vaccine.

INDIGENOUS
People, plants or animals that are native to the region or country in which they are living.

MIGRANT
Anybody who moves to another region or country, temporarily or permanently, for whatever reason.

NOMADIC
Following a way of life that requires moving from one location to another, without a settled home. Nomadic peoples include hunters and gatherers, herders of sheep or cattle and traders.

PEOPLE TRAFFICKERS
Criminals who exploit people for profit, often for forced labour, sexual slavery or illegal migration.

POPULATION DENSITY
A measurement of the number of people living within a unit area.

POPULATION GROWTH RATE
The increase of a population, as a proportion of the total, within a given time frame, for example 2 per cent per year.

PREJUDICE
An unfavourable opinion already formed without due consideration of the facts.

PUBLIC HEALTH
The general health of the population as a whole.

RACE
A classification of humans by their appearance, ancestry or culture.

RACISM
The belief that humans can be classed by race, and that some races are superior to others.

REFUGEE
Somebody who flees their home, generally because of war, persecution or a natural disaster.

REPRODUCTIVE RIGHTS
The rights of the individual to have children or not, to access sex education and health services, to prevent or end a pregnancy.

SHANTYTOWN
Sprawling, makeshift housing or slums around a big city. Other words include favela or bidonville.

SHAREHOLDERS
People who invest money in a company in return for owning part, or a share of it.

SMOG
A toxic mixture of smoke, pollutants or other emissions which creates a haze or fog over a city.

STABILISATION
Becoming steadier, levelling off.

STERILISATION
Making someone unable to conceive, by surgical or chemical treatment.

SUSTAINABLE
Able to be maintained in the long term.

TERMINATION
The act of ending something, another word for abortion.

TRANSNATIONAL
Of corporations, based in several countries and operating internationally.

URBANISATION
A movement of people from the countryside into towns and cities.

INDEX

PICTURE CREDITS